BTS
Making a Difference as a Band

By Katie Kawa

People Who Make a Difference

KidHaven PUBLISHING

Published in 2023 by
KidHaven Publishing, an Imprint of Greenhaven Publishing, LLC
29 E. 21st Street
New York, NY 10010

Designer: Deanna Paternostro
Editor: Katie Kawa

Photo credits: Cover Silvia Elizabeth Pangaro/Shutterstock.com; p. 5 Kathy Hutchins/Shutterstock.com; p. 7 Featureflash Photo Agency/Shutterstock.com; pp. 9, 17 ZUMA Press, Inc./Alamy Stock Photo; p. 11 Erik Pendzich/Alamy Stock Photo; p. 13 Sipa USA/Alamy Stock Photo; p. 15 AP Photo/Craig Ruttle; p. 18 AP Photo/Lee Jin-man; p. 20 Everett Collection Inc/Alamy Stock Photo; p. 21 T.Sumaetho/Shutterstock.com.

Library of Congress Cataloging-in-Publication Data

Names: Kawa, Katie, author.
Title: BTS : making a difference as a band / Katie Kawa.
Description: [First.] | New York : KidHaven Publishing, 2023. | Series: People who make a difference | Includes index.
Identifiers: LCCN 2021056399 | ISBN 9781534541665 (set) | ISBN 9781534541672 (library binding) | ISBN 9781534541658 (paperback) | ISBN 9781534541689 (ebook)
Subjects: LCSH: BTS (Musical group)–Juvenile literature. | Singers–Korea (South)–Biography–Juvenile literature. | Rock musicians–Korea (South)–Biography–Juvenile literature. | Boy bands–Korea (South)–Juvenile literature.
Classification: LCC ML3930.B89 K38 2023 | DDC 782.4216/3095195 [B]–dc23
LC record available at https://lccn.loc.gov/2021056399

Printed in the United States of America

CPSIA compliance information: Batch #CSKH23: For further information contact Greenhaven Publishing LLC, New York, New York at 1-844-317-7404.

Please visit our website, www.greenhavenpublishing.com. For a free color catalog of all our high-quality books, call toll free 1-844-317-7404 or fax 1-844-317-7405.

CONTENTS

A UNIVERSAL LANGUAGE

Music is sometimes called a universal language. This means it's something that speaks to everyone around the world. People from different countries, backgrounds, and ways of life can all be brought together by music.

One band that's bringing people together using this universal language is BTS. This group of seven men from South Korea has become one of the most popular bands in the world. No matter what language they're singing in, they **inspire** their fans with an important message: Love yourself. BTS is making a difference with their music, and it's a difference that's being felt around the world!

In Their Words

"If there's something I can do, if our voices can give strength to people, then that's what we want, and that's what we'll keep on doing."

— Jung Kook, speaking in a video for the **United Nations** (UN) in September 2020

The members of BTS are (from left to right): V (Kim Tae-hyung), Suga (Min Yoon-gi), Jin (Kim Seok-jin), Jung Kook (Jeon Jung-kook), RM (Kim Nam-joon), Jimin (Park Ji-min), and J-Hope (Jung Ho-seok). They're best known by their stage names—names they use when they're **performing**.

THE BAND'S BEGINNING

The members of BTS were all born in the 1990s. Jin was born in 1992, Suga in 1993, J-Hope and RM in 1994, Jimin and V in 1995, and Jung Kook in 1997. They grew up in different parts of South Korea and didn't come together as a band until the 2010s.

In 2010, RM was asked to be a part of a new music group. Over time, the other members joined, and in 2013, BTS debuted, or officially put out their first songs as a group. Their first **single album**, *2 Cool 4 Skool*, came out on June 12, 2013.

In Their Words

"I always wanted to become an artist that can provide comfort … and positive energy [feelings] to people."

— J-Hope, in an interview with *TIME* magazine from December 2020

BTS is often called a K-pop group. K-pop is style of popular, or pop, music from South Korea, and K-pop songs are often performed in Korean. Some K-pop bands have rappers, and BTS has three! RM, Suga, and J-Hope are known for their rapping skills.

MAKING MUSIC

Fame didn't come right away for BTS. They had to work hard for it. They released, or put out, two more short albums before their first full-length album, *Dark & Wild*, was released in 2014. Between 2015 and 2016, they released three albums in a trilogy, or set of three, called *The Most Beautiful Moment in Life Trilogy* (or the *Youth Trilogy*).

In fall 2016, BTS came out with their second full-length album, *Wings*. The next year, they added more songs to *Wings* and gave it a new title: *You Never Walk Alone*. By 2017, BTS was winning **awards** in Asia and the United States.

In Their Words

"Any moment can be turned into an opportunity. Allow yourself to take it easy. Take it one step at a time."

— Jin, speaking in a video to **graduates** in 2020

BTS has been busy making music ever since they debuted in 2013. They've also made albums in Japanese, and some BTS members have released music on their own too.

SHARING THEIR STORIES

Between 2017 and 2018, BTS released another trilogy of albums: *Love Yourself: Her*, *Love Yourself: Tear*, and *Love Yourself: Answer*. They followed that trilogy with *Map of the Soul: Persona* in 2019 and *Map of the Soul: 7* in 2020.

The members of BTS write a lot of their own music, and they often write about problems young people face. As they've gotten older, they've become even more open in their music, interviews, and social media posts about their **mental** health. By sharing their struggles with mental health conditions such as **depression**, they help their fans who are struggling feel less alone.

In Their Words

"Those sort of negative emotions [feelings] come and go. For anybody, these emotions are not things that need to be hidden. They need to be … expressed [shared]. Whatever emotions I may be feeling, I'm always ready to express them."

— Suga, in an interview with *Rolling Stone* magazine from May 2021

The members of BTS talk openly about their mental health and how much they care about each other. Many people say that by doing these things, they're showing others, especially other men and boys, that it's good to talk about your feelings.

LOVE MYSELF

It isn't always easy to love yourself, even if you're a member of one of the biggest bands in the world. However, the members of BTS know that loving yourself is important. That's the message behind their song "Answer: Love Myself" from the *Love Yourself: Answer* album. In this song, BTS tells their fans, "You've shown me I have reasons / I should love myself."

BTS has spread this message around the world. In 2017, the band began working with UNICEF—the part of the UN that helps children. While working with UNICEF, they created the LOVE MYSELF **campaign** to inspire people to love themselves and others.

In Their Words

"I realized that we've been telling people to really love themselves and telling them to be stronger. This year, I began to tell *myself* these things as well, and convincing [showing] myself that this is also something I need to keep in mind."

— Jimin, in an interview with *Rolling Stone* magazine from May 2021

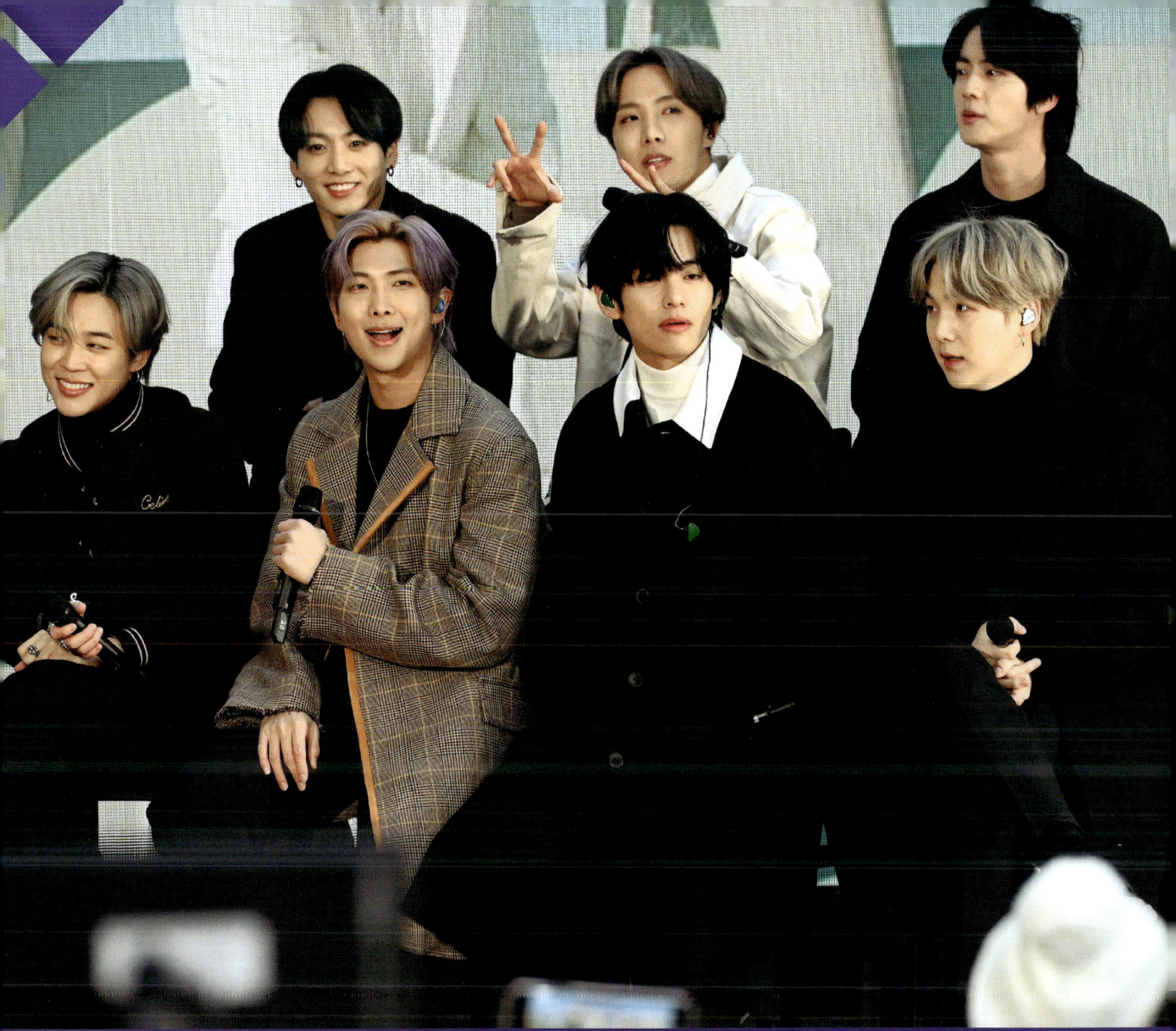

BTS's work with UNICEF also deals with ending **violence** against children and teens. They want to help build a world where young people feel safe, loved, and supported.

"SPEAK YOURSELF"

BTS has helped raise millions of dollars through the LOVE MYSELF campaign. They've also inspired young people to share stories of their journeys toward loving themselves.

The members of BTS have shared their stories in a very important way. In September 2018, they traveled to New York City to speak in front of the UN General Assembly—the part of the UN that makes policies, or plans for taking action. RM delivered a speech there about the need to "speak yourself"—to share your story with the world. BTS returned to New York City to give another speech in 2021 about issues that matter to young people.

In Their Words

"Tell me your story. I want to hear your voice … No matter who you are, where you're from, your skin color, your **gender identity**—speak yourself."

— RM, speaking before the UN General Assembly in September 2018

BTS is shown here at the UN in 2018. In 2021, they returned as Special Presidential Envoys for Future Generations and Culture. This title was given to them by South Korea's president. Their job is to represent, or stand for, South Korea on the world stage, especially when dealing with issues that young people care about.

GIVING BACK

The members of BTS have other causes that are close to their hearts too. They've given money to schools in the towns and cities where they grew up. They've also given money to museums, hospitals, and schools that help students with hearing difficulties. In addition, they donated, or gave, $1 million to the Black Lives Matter organization in 2020. This group works to fight **racism** and violence against Black people.

BTS's fans, known as ARMY, matched that $1 million and even went beyond it. They've been inspired by BTS to raise money for many different causes. BTS has said that ARMY inspires them too!

In Their Words

"Things may feel a little difficult [hard] right now, but somewhere out there, luck and opportunity is waiting for you."

— V, speaking in a video to graduates in 2020

BTS finds many ways to stay connected to their fans—whether it's through their web series and TV shows such as *Run BTS* and *In the Soop*, concerts that are in person or online, or social media posts. They often say they want their fans to be happy and healthy, and they make sure their fans know they care about them.

A HARD YEAR

BTS was ready to go on a world tour in 2020, but then the **COVID-19 pandemic** happened. They had to cancel their tour. The members of the band missed performing for their fans, and some of them have talked about being depressed during this time. This was a hard time for people around the world, and BTS's honesty helped their fans feel understood.

BTS used their time during the pandemic to make new music. Their album *Be* came out in 2020. They also released three songs in English between 2020 and 2021: "Dynamite," "Butter," and "Permission to Dance." They wanted these songs to spread joy.

In Their Words

"Stars shine brightest when the night is darkest."

— RM, speaking in a video for the UN in September 2020

The Story of BTS

1992
Jin is born.

1993
Suga is born.

1994
J-Hope and RM are born.

1995
Jimin and V are born.

1997
Jung Kook is born.

2010
The creation of BTS begins when RM is asked to be part of a music group.

2013
BTS debuts with their single album *2 Cool for Skool.*

2014
BTS releases their first full-length album, *Dark & Wild.*

2016
BTS releases their second full-length album, *Wings.*

2017
BTS releases the album *You Never Walk Alone* and begins working with UNICEF.

2018
BTS releases the album *Love Yourself: Answer.* RM speaks before the UN General Assembly.

2020
The albums *Map of the Soul: 7* and *Be* are released, and "Dynamite" becomes a worldwide hit.

2021
"Butter" and "Permission to Dance" are released, and BTS plays their first concerts in two years in Los Angeles, California.

BTS has worked hard for many years to find success in South Korea and around the world. In 2020 and 2021, their songs became huge hits in the United States!

LOOKING UP

The COVID-19 pandemic made it hard for BTS to see their fans. However, things started looking up at the end of 2021. In November and December, BTS had four concerts in Los Angeles, California. They finally got to see their fans in person, and their fans got to connect with each other too.

BTS makes music to connect with their fans and to help them in hard times. They want to help their fans love themselves, and they've done this by sharing their own stories, especially in their songs. They're using the universal language of music to make the world a better place!

In Their Words

"Please use me. Please use BTS to love yourself—because you guys taught me how to love myself every day."

— RM, speaking to fans at a concert in New York City in 2018

Be Like BTS!

Raise money for causes you care about.

Tell the people you love that you love them—and tell yourself too!

Help your friends and family love themselves by reminding them of all the things you love about them.

Listen respectfully and show kindness when someone talks to you about their mental health, and be honest with a trusted adult if you're feeling sad or lonely.

Write down a list of things you like about yourself, and read them on days when loving yourself feels hard.

If you're having a hard time, write down what you're feeling. If you feel comfortable, share it with someone you trust so they can help.

If you know someone who's having a hard time, write something to cheer them up or to inspire them to feel better about themselves. It could be a song, a poem, or a card.

BTS has used their talents to spread a message of love around the world. Here are some ways you can share this message with the people around you!

GLOSSARY

award: A prize given for doing something well.
campaign: A set of activities or events meant to produce a certain result.
COVID-19 pandemic: An event that began in China in 2019 in which a disease that causes breathing problems, a fever, and other health issues spread rapidly around the world and made millions of people sick in a short period of time.
depression: A mental health condition in which a person feels very sad, hopeless, and unimportant and is often unable to do basic tasks because of this.
gender identity: A person's own sense of being male, female, some combination of the two, or neither male nor female.
graduate: A person who has finished the required course of study in a school.
inspire: To move someone to do something great.
mental: Relating to the mind.
perform: To entertain people by singing, acting, or doing some other activity that requires skill.
racism: The practice of treating others poorly because they are part of a different race, or group of people who look alike in certain ways. This word also relates to governments and societies that allow one race to be treated better than others.
single album: An album that has a very small number of songs on it.
United Nations: An organization formed in 1945 to promote international cooperation.
violence: The use of force to harm someone.

FOR MORE INFORMATION

WEBSITES

BTS

ibighit.com/bts/eng/

This is the official website (in English) of BTS, featuring facts about their albums, the story of the band, and links to the band's social media pages.

LOVE MYSELF

www.love-myself.org/eng/home

This website features facts about BTS's LOVE MYSELF campaign, videos with the members of the band, and a timeline of the campaign's biggest moments.

BOOKS

Croft, Malcolm. *BTS: The Ultimate Fan Book: Experience the K-Pop Phenomenon!* London, UK: Carlton Books, 2019.

Croft, Malcolm. *K-Pop: The Ultimate Fan Book: Your Essential Guide to All the Hottest K-Pop Bands*. New York, NY: Sterling Children's Books, 2019.

Stevens, Cara J. *BTS: Rise of Bangtan*. New York, NY: HarperCollins, 2018.

Publisher's note to educators and parents: Our editors have carefully reviewed these websites to ensure that they are suitable for students. Many websites change frequently, however, and we cannot guarantee that a site's future contents will continue to meet our high standards of quality and educational value. Be advised that students should be closely supervised whenever they access the Internet.

INDEX